Investing in **Real Estate**

Finding the perfect **Building**
Getting a Good **Deal**
Adding **Value**

bricoarts.com

Preface

I thank my family for all their support and guidance during this journey

I also thank my friends and God for all the light, faith and love

Introduction

Every investment has its risks.

The purpose of this book is to help you identify and manage them as much as possible.

Buildings, along with food and energy, are some of the essentials we need for our survival and prosperity. It is thus logic to assume they are, and always will be, an excellent investment.

Whether you aim to refurbish your buildings, buy new ones or old ones, live in them, rent them or sell them, this book will show you how to carefully plan your steps along the way and make the most of the process of adding value to your properties.

Thank you for choosing this book, I wish these guidelines help you make great investments and lead you to a happy and prosperous life.

Godspeed!

Step 1 | Location

The first thing to consider when investing in real estate, whether it is a site or a building, is its location. It is important to choose a place with activity, lots of people and business and nearby public facilities and transports. Where there are people and businesses, there is value and money.

I advise you to study a map of the city or area where you want to invest, preferably a satellite view, and add pins to the most important business centers and public facilities in that area, such as universities, hospitals and public administration. You will be looking for buildings and activities that will remain there for a lot of time and that add value to their communities and surroundings. After you identified some zones, ideally neighborhood size in radius, or streets (some important commerce and business tend to run in an axis shape like streets) it is time to hit the road.

First drive around and study parking spaces and access to highways and other infrastructures for mobility. Then park your car and walk around talking to people like neighbors and workers. Walking and talking is the best way to sense a place and get real feedback from it.

Trust your gut, if you sense something isn't right, try to identify what it is, and after you have rationalized it make a decision. Some places are apparently perfect, others awful, but the underlying truth and energy of a place goes way beyond appearances.

Sometimes a place or a building can look a mess, but neighbors are nice and friendly, like in my recent investment in a neighborhood's old house from 1930. It was in ruins and many people advised me not to buy it, but the more I talked to neighbors and felt the site the more I felt it was a great investment. It was located in a quiet place behind the local shopping center, nearby hospital and street market, in the entrance of the city from the highway.

Despite the ruins feel to this house and others in the neighborhood, it had potential, and other investors are now doing the same refurbishing nearby houses.

So first step: walk & talk.

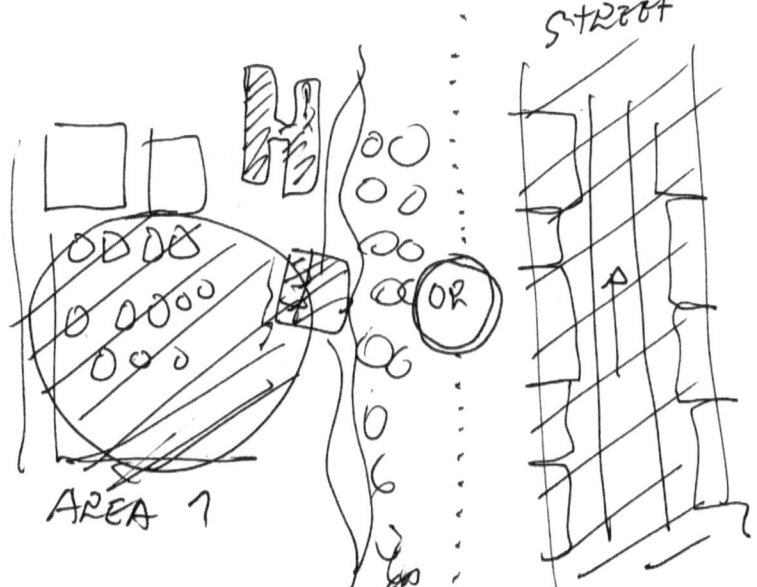

AREA 1 / OR / STREET

Step 2 | A Good Deal

After choosing a location its time to find a good deal. Good deals come in many forms, sometimes ruins are great deals, because most people want to buy the "cooked thing". Building new or rebuilding takes a lot of energy, time and money, and most people just want to buy the ready thing, even if it means being tied to a heavy loan for their entire lives.

I recommend investing with your own money or savings, only buying credit in an emergency or in case your construction surpasses initial costs. This way you will buy what you need and can afford, not an illusion or an overpriced building.This path of investment isn´t easy or magical, it takes energy and resilience, but every human being is born with those skills, so its a matter of will and faith.

Back to the deal, a ruin or old building is usually a good deal, but you need to factor in the money necessary for the reconstruction. In order to keep your numbers in control I advise creating a spreadsheet with the following items:

1 | Base Cost of the Building or Site

2 | Land Site Square Meters

3 | Construction Square meters

4 | Land Cost per Square Meter

5 | Construction Cost per Square Meter

6 | Total Investment

The key is to look online for many buildings or sites for sale in that area and find the average cost per square meter, that is the average value of the real estate. If the real-estate you want is above average, it could be a bad deal.

Next talk to friends and contractors to find out the average cost per square meter to refurbish or build your construction. Multiply that by the area of your building and you will find the average sum for the investment.

You need to be careful here. A construction is a tricky process, there are many unforeseen surprises along the way, especially in old buildings. To account for these I recommend a 20% margin on top of the construction investment budget, just to be prepared. In my investment the roof was in a worse shape that I anticipated and the global cost increased around 20%.

In fact, the roof and the structure of the building should be your main concerns. This is where you will get a good deal, you will be buying a site that already comes with a structure and a roof! If you choose a more safer approach, such as an apartment, store or office in a bigger building, be careful to check if there are major repairs to be made, on the roof, facades, elevators and plumbing and electrical services.

These days most real estate for sale is online, but sometimes doing the walk and talk you may find excellent deals. I remember to have put business letters and cards in old houses with my contact saying: "I would like to buy this house, please call me or email me. Thank you."

If you're going to a real estate consultant, look for the best ones, but remember most willl try to sell you anything, anywhere. So be clear where you want to invest and what you are looking for: such as an old house up to ___m2 under _____€ in the _____ area.

I believe old houses, ruins, empty stores, offices and warehouses to be excellent deals these days. Mainly because people don't want old things and are afraid of construction works. In a present sustainable approach, refurbishing and reusing something that is old is also interesting and makes perfect sense in countries where population is aging and newborns diminishing.

So get out there, and good luck finding your deal. Remember to be patient, it usually takes 3 to 6 months to find the perfect building.

Step 3 | Design Scheme

After finding and buying your property its time to find an architect. You might think you don't need one, because you already know what you want and the contractor can help you, but here are some thoughts on what architects do:

1 | They help you write the functional program you need and want

2 | They listen to you and help you design the building of your dreams

3 | They guard your interests when dealing with contractors and sellers

4 | They are there for you and reassure you during the whole construction process

5 | They will advise you about maintenance and care during the lifespan of your building

A design scheme begins with a site survey, measurements must be made to assist in the design process. With accurate measurements we will produce accurate designs, interior divisions and quantify materials.

After inserting the measurements in a design software, an architect will begin to study interior layouts and show you several distribution options. For a while it is good to exchange ideas with family and friends but there will come a point when a layout must be decided.

These days open spaces are a trend, they maximize space and light while reducing construction and maintenance costs. So halls, corridors and multiple doors are beginning to give place to open spaces.

An architect will also integrate structures and electrical and mechanical services into your design, so that there are no surprises in construction. The job of an architect is to integrate all your needs with the structure, building services and other conditions in an aesthetic way. That said, solving construction problems in a pleasant visual fashion. Architects will also design the exterior of the building at the same time they integrate the other criteria, its like creating a product from scratch, everything must work together as both a whole and a sum of individual parts, like a maestro writing and conducting a play.

The fun part is you can write and conduct the play together.

Good luck finding your architect!

Step 4 | Budgeting

Budgeting is the most important step of your investment.

A team of an architect and an engineer can assist you in quantifying your construction investment. Bear in mind that most professionals will use prices databases, for materials and services, so remind to factor those 20% extra on top of that.

Ideally if you get discounts shopping around and find cheap contractors, the final construction cost might be smaller than your initial budget, but that is harder than winning the lottery!

I recommend writing down your budget in a spreadsheet in order, although there are other valid templates around, quantities in this link model are references from other works while prices will vary depending on your location.

https://drive.google.com/drive/folders/1jIKayLHlc9VR40bUiiFUvYuwsfd_IXan?usp=drive_link

Do remember to add 20% on top of the total value as a safety margin. This way you will be better prepared to face unforeseen problems. Back in the nineteen hundreds my grandfather was a global contractor and he used to say a construction was like a pregnant lady, you never knew how many children she would have. Today we have computers, softwares and databases to help us, nevertheless keeping a safety margin is always better than getting an unpleasant surprise.

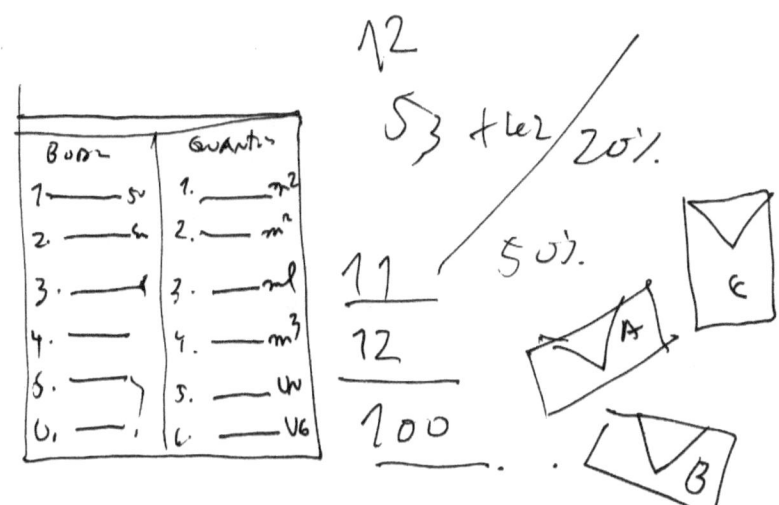

Step 5 | Shopping for Materials

After you have your budgets and quantities takeoffs, it's time to go shopping around.

Again your architect can help you find good materials and prices. The architect will help you find the best stores for your construction. An architect will also help you will detect any flaws or problems with a specific material.

Usually basic materials like cement, bricks, sand, gravel and insulation can be purchased in generic stores. Some stores will have better prices in claddings, ceramics, paints and finishings. Other stores will have better prices in woods while others in hardwares and metals and others in electrical or plumbing equipments. So it's important to shop around for every kind of material, this way you will save a lot of money.

If you like to do some construction works yourself, always remember to buy and wear safety gear. Sometimes in your free time it can be nice to walk around hardware stores and check out tools and materials, comparing prices and features!

Finally when cutting the deal it is always better to pay upfront, this way you will get even better prices than if you pay later or with credit. You can also have your materials delivered at your construction site saving you a lot of time.

Step 6 | Hiring Contractors

H iring contractors and other construction services can be done in 2 ways:

1 | Hiring a Global Contractor, that will be in charge of all subcontractors and services

2 | Hiring every Contractor in separate

Option 1 saves you a lot of stress and time but comes at an extra price. Since the global contractor will be in charge of every worker in your construction, that work will cost you an extra.

Option 2 can save you a lot of money and you can handle it in two fashions, either hiring an architect or an engineer to manage and coordinate everyone, or doing it yourself.

Managing a construction can be a very stressful operation, especially if you don't understand technical and professional construction matters. Some people do it, but to survive the process a lot of assertiveness and patience will be required.

Regarding budgets and prices, it is advisable to ask up to 3 budgets from different contractors for the tasks. More than 3 budgets generates confusion and is unfair for the people who dedicate their time providing those budgets.

In refurbishing I recommend hiring professionals on a daily basis. Reach an agreement on a fair value to pay per day per worker and pay them at the end of every week. This way everyone builds trust and work is fair and accounts for surprises during the process.

A fixed budget can be good for a new construction, where most works can be predicted. In a refurbishment however, there will be many surprises along the way, so if a contractor is asked to provide a fixed budget he will protect himself by raising his price to account for those surprises. On a daily budget mode everyone is safe and free to walk away anytime if their objectives aren't met.

There are many professionals available, the most important qualities to look for are trust and care for detail. Not necessarily price, because many times a 20% cheaper professional will require a 30% or more extra surveillance and corrections, so price is very relative.

Trustful and professional people who answer your calls and return them during the day, that show up when they say they will and that have a positive attitude towards the works and other subcontractors will be your top pick.

Contractors are the people who will make your dreams real, material, so they must always be rewarded for that and be treated with respect, especially when handling problems.

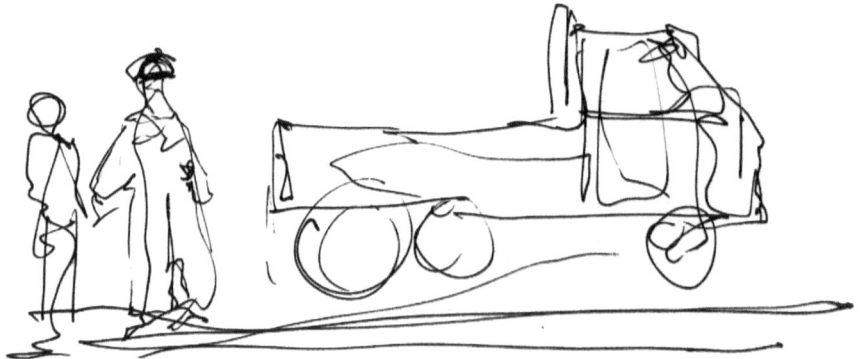

Step 7 | Managing the Construction

Managing a construction really comes down to the 2 options mentioned in Step 6:

1 | Hiring a Global Contractor: he will be in charge of all subcontractors and services

2 | Hiring every contractor in separate: you will be managing all subcontractors and services

If you have a lot of money and little time, go for option 1, you probably make more money dedicating your time to your work and business than the money you will save managing a construction. If on the other hand you have a lot of time but little money, choosing option 2 can save you from 20% to 50% in some contractor services and 20% to 60% in some materials costs.

You will need to be calm and assertive, the most difficult task will be dealing with people, dealing with the construction and its problems will be simple compared to that.

If you happen to like doing bricolage and construction works, you can also save a lot of money in exchange for your time. Always remember to wear protection gear and previously study the tasks you will be performing. Choose those tasks carefully, based on your skills and experience. While some tasks appear simple, doing them can be extremely difficult.

I personally find demolitions, building walls and rough floors to be possible tasks to achieve with some level of quality. I recommend hiring professionals to do finishings, like ceramics, woods and paints as well as electrical and water fixtures. Some mistakes cannot be fixed, bearing high time and material losses, so choose the tasks you will perform wisely.

If at some point you feel exhausted, give yourself a treat. Let go of that stress doing something you love or take some time away from the site. On a daily basis that can be achieved going for walks or meals, buying materials, meeting friends. When you come back to the site you will find your new fresh mind essential to handle the problems!

Remember people are emotional beings, work on empathy and leadership, there are many books around to help you build assertiveness, empathy, leadership and other skills.

An intermediate approach to option 2 would be hiring an architect or an engineer to manage the construction for you. You will find his cost will still be cheaper than option's 1 extra price, however you will still need to meet with him and visit the construction quite often.

The perfect choice is Option 1 with an Architect managing the whole construction process, an expensive process that will save you a lot of stress.

The decision comes down to knowing how much your time and stress are worth. Whatever path you choose, you already have the skills and tools you need to face it. When you begin to see the building gain shape you will gain fresh confidence and joy and when the building is complete, you will be rewarded with an extraordinary legacy.

Step 8 | Renting or Selling

After you have finished your building its time to plan if you're going to rent it or sell it.

Real estate markets fluctuates like any market, prices go up and down depending on the demand and the economy. It´s common sense to think that buying cheap and selling expensive is a good deal, however there are better times to buy and better times to sell.

Usually when there is a lot of offer and the economy is down its a good time to buy since most people will be looking to make cash. When there is a lot of demand and the economy is back up, especially now when credits interests are at a historically low and savings interests are also historically low, it's a great time to sell.

At present date real estate value is rising a one digit percent every year, so the trick is to predict when will it stop rising and when will it start declining. I am an architect, not an economist, but it appears interest rates are good data as well as employment and internal growth.

It is wise to collaborate with Real estate agents, Contractors, Industrial Leaders and Commerce Owners to feel the economy's heartbeat. This way you will be able to sense the "weather". If you are a more conservative and careful investor or you don't need the money for other businesses, renting is a good option. As with selling always talk to an accountant to check the amount of money you will pay in taxes so you have your numbers solid and working for you.

Renting comes down to a good contract that protects your interests, so seek out a lawyer to help you with that, in case you need the house for yourself or you want to sell it one day your contract must account for that. Short term rental, or "airbnb", can be interesting but it's a lot of work. To get a higher return than long term rental one needs to manage the property oneself, including cleaning and laundry. It does have the advantage of regular turnover and maintenance that long term renting does not, therefore keeping the house in better condition. Usually houses that have more than 2 bedrooms are candidates for parties and damage, be mindful of all the risks and talk to other short term rentals in your area for specifics.

On long term and mid term rentals, a good real estate agent can help you get a great deal since they have many contacts. The internet is also a good option to advertise your property, but again it will be up to you to show the building and hear complaints and negative feedback that buyers and renters will throw at you to get a better deal.

Good fortune!

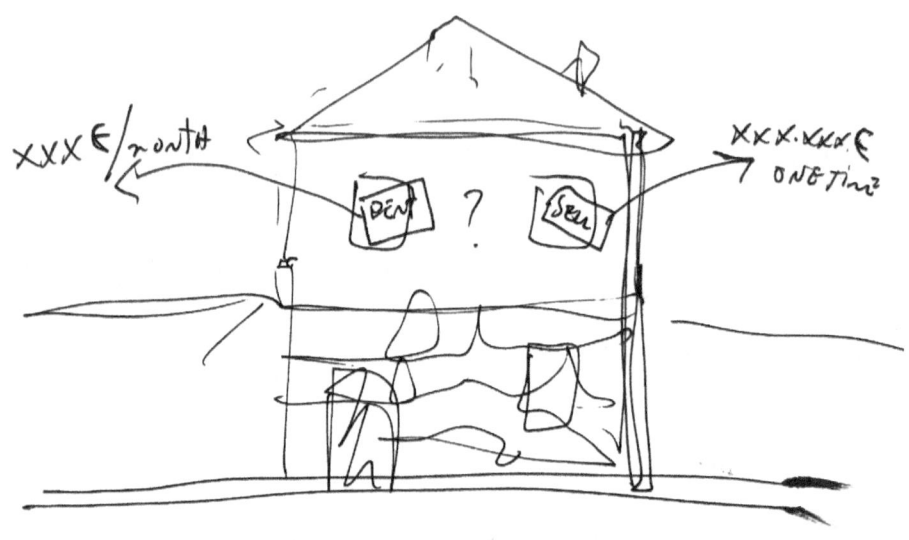

Conclusion

Adding value to a building or a business requires a lot of time, energy and money. This means work is necessary to add value to property. It may be intellectual, physical or a combination of both. Sometimes there are strokes of luck, but even luck has to be caught for it walks the streets randomly. I wish this book truly helps you take action and improve your real estate portfolio and your life. I thank you for buying this book, you are always welcome to visit us at bricoarts.com

Feel free to download free guides and templates at:

https://drive.google.com/drive/folders/1jIKayLHIc9VR40bUiiFUvYuwsfd_IXan?usp=drive_link

Have a great year!

www.ingramcontent.com/pod-product-compliance
Lightning Source LLC
Chambersburg PA
CBHW031526210526
45464CB00007B/3029